The Sacral Chakra is our Water Center. It holds the urinary tract, bladder, kidneys and sexual organs. It's the site of our preferences, where our likes and our dislikes begin. Called Swadisthana, this second chakra is also how we birth ourselves, our children and our values into the world. How we give and how we receive, how we experience intimacy with others, ourselves and the Divine.

The Water Center wants what it wants, regardless of what society tells us we "should" want. Repressing those deep longings and preferences doesn't make them go away. It just forces them to express in other ways. They can turn inward or outward, but when we fail to honor the Second Chakra, desire escapes our conscious influence. When frustrated, desire can turn into pain, grief, guilt and anger. Misdirected creativity creates disease and symptoms instead of the things we most desire.

This guided recovery workbook evolved from 18 years as a Medical Intuitive and is written to help you reclaim your Sacral Chakra. It supports different levels of the healing process, but is not intended to replace medical or other therapeutic advice. By reading and responding to these questions, you accept responsibility for your own journey, and the author disclaims all liability. Your answers are yours and yours alone. They may shift as the questions shift, and some later questions sound similar to earlier ones, to allow for changing answers as you heal. All questions are copyrighted to Laura Bruno, 2019. All rights reserved.

In love and joy, I wish you well.

Laura Bruno

http://asklaurabruno.com

1. What signs, song lyrics, or synchronicities have you noticed lately? Have you had any recurring "random" thoughts, conversations or dreams? What small details suggest a larger theme?

2. What does your primal inner knowing tell you that you need for your recovery? How can you address these needs? What small step(s) can you take towards listening to and honoring your primal inner knowing?

3. What skills, talents, attitudes, personality traits, and/or gifts do you already have, and which new ones are you developing? What's "right" with you? Take inventory and offer thanks.

4. What small things bring you great satisfaction? What "little" things piss you off? Which small daily or weekly steps would allow you to experience more satisfaction and less annoyance?

5. Make a list of words and ideas you associate with water. Record whatever ideas cross your mind, no limits. You can also draw, paint, write a poem, or make a collage.

6. Explore your relationship with the Element of Water. Do you crave it or avoid it? Which qualities of water could you benefit from having more of in your life? Which qualities of water detract from your experience of life?

7a. How does your relationship with the Element of Water influence your experience of things like flow, boundaries, emotions, intuition, and empathic awareness?

7b. What could you do to bring more balance to the Element of Water in your life?

8a. Which do you like best: waterfall, lake, pond, stream, river, bay, ocean, bath, shower, or a hot tub? What does your answer tell you about your preferred relationship with water?

8b. How does your preferred relationship with water play out in your life? In which ways do you honor or avoid water in this form? What might this form represent for you in terms of life situations and relationships?

9. If you were a water creature - real or mythical - what would you be and why?

10. What do you long to create? What wants to flow through you? Do you make time for creative expression? What small habits, disciplines or practices would encourage more creative output?

11. How can you bring more beauty and harmony into your life? How can you bring more beauty and harmony into the world?

12a. Make a list of words and ideas you associate with fire. Record whatever ideas cross your mind, no limits. You can also draw, paint, write a poem, or make a collage

12b. Explore your relationship with the Element of Fire. Do you crave it or avoid it? Which qualities of fire could you benefit from having more of in your life? Which qualities of fire detract from your experience of life?

13a. How does your relationship with the Element of Fire influence your experience of things like passion, anger, frustration, productivity, procrastination, and determination?

13b. What could you do to bring more balance to the Element of Fire in your life?

14. If you were a fire symbol or creature - real or mythical - what would you be and why?

15a. How do you experience anger in yourself and others? Is it repressed or overwhelming? Hot? Cold? Volatile? Resentful? Annoyed? Raging? Is anger a friend, enemy or something else? Why?

15b. In what ways does anger scare you? How do you express anger? How and where does unexpressed anger affect your body? If you don't know, just write the first answer that comes to mind and explore that answer.

16a. Which people and/or situations irritate you? Don't censor your response. This question is for you and you alone to answer. Be thorough.

16b. Choose the most irritating person or situation in your life to work with here. In one word, what does this person/situation represent for you? In one word, what's the feeling behind your first answer? In one word, what's the feeling behind your second answer? Explore this second feeling and its implications.

17a. What little, seemingly insignificant things bother you a lot? What big things feel out of your control?

17b. Choose a small, irritating situation or circumstance of life to address. List three shifts you could make to eliminate or minimize exposure to this irritant. Which small step(s) will you take to improve this area of your life?

18. In which ways do you honor commitments to others more than you honor commitments to yourself? Why do you prioritize others' needs above your own needs?

19a. What does "Respect, Not Control" mean to you? How do these concepts affect your relationships, for better or worse?

19b. Do you aim for respect, control, or a combination? Why or why not?

20. When you compare yourself to others, how do you feel? In which areas of your life and body do you feel comparisons? Which habits or situations trigger comparisons or judgment?

21a. What thoughts, emotions, foods, attitudes and/or situations trigger increased symptoms? What themes and patterns do you notice in this list?

21b. Are these things new in your life, or amplified old themes and patterns? Under what circumstances did they first begin?

22. If symptoms were guiding you to improve your life, towards which directions and decisions would fewer symptoms point?

23a. Which relationships demand more of you than you receive in return? Is this a temporary, new development, or a long term pattern? Describe the dynamics.

23b. How do imbalanced relationships affect your symptoms, energy, and emotions?

23c. What's in it for you? This is not a rhetorical question. Be honest with yourself: what benefit do you receive from imbalanced relationships? If you receive no benefit, then why do you remain in this relationship?

24. What relationship boundaries or support do you need for your healing?

25. What would help you to feel more empowered on your healing journey?

26a. Do you ever feel guilty about taking time to care for yourself? Why or why not?

26b. What small steps or personal mantras would help you to feel more balanced and supported?

27. Check in with yourself again. Make a list of any gifts, talents, skills, supportive relationships, or other blessings that you have right now. What's right with you? What's right with your life? Take stock and offer thanks.

28a. Have you ever been sexually harassed or sexually abused? If so, do you feel you've healed from this? What other kinds of abuse or boundary violations have you experienced?

28b. Do you feel supported to move through these abuse or boundary issues? If not, what kind of support would help you to heal on the physical, mental, emotional, and spiritual levels?

29a. What would you need in order to forgive your abuser and yourself? Do you believe you will ever receive this?

29b. How will you know when it's safe to forgive? Does forgiveness mean forgetting? (These are not rhetorical questions: answer honestly for you, as you feel right now.)

30a. Name something for which you feel guilty or ashamed. At that time and that level of awareness, what other options did you have? Why did you choose as you did?

30b. What pieces of you remain linked to guilt or shame? Before you go to sleep tonight, intend and ask your subconscious mind to reclaim any pieces of your soul stuck in that old experience.

31a. Who or what annoys you and why? Big or small, politically correct or not, be honest.

31b. In a perfect world, what changes would feel like welcome upgrades? What small, achievable step(s) would help you move in the direction of relief?

32. What does your intuition tell you that you need for your recovery? Have these needs changed or remained constant? How can you address these needs? What small step(s) can you take towards following your intuition today? This week? This month?

33. What gets you excited in a happy way? What brings you joy? What surprises you about these answers?

34. Do you feel embarrassed or comfortable with desire, excitement, happiness and joy? Answer separately for each emotion if your answers differ. What blocks or openings do your answers suggest?

35. How do other people's emotions or health issues affect you? Do you feel them in your own moods or body? Ask yourself, "Is this mine?" Always pay attention to the answer. Record your answers here so you remember them.

36a. Black tourmaline, sea salt, charoite, and hematite crystals all offer protection for empaths. What other tools, crystals, mantras, habits or techniques help you to create an energetic and emotional buffer?

36b. What habits or addictions do you use to tune out, numb out or keep other people's energies from overwhelming you? How could you replace or upgrade these with something more positive and healing?

37. How have intimate relationships helped or hindered your healing journey? In what ways has their help or hinderance made you stronger?

38. What does your healing journey ask you to release? What does your healing journey ask you to receive?

39. How do you feel about sex? Would you like more or less of it? If you had to choose a metaphor for your sex life right now, what would it be? How does that metaphor make you feel?

40a. How do you feel about masturbation? Does it "work" for you? What feelings does it bring up? (Relaxation? Love? Frustration? Anger? Peace? Shame?) Be honest.

40b. How do you feel about pleasing yourself in other ways? What, if any, differences do you notice between your attitudes towards autoerotic sexual pleasure or nonsexual pleasure? How do these attitudes influence your approach to living a satisfying life?

41. Do you feel free to express yourself in a sexual or sensual way? What's the difference between sexual and sensual? Do you prefer one over the other? Neither? Both? Why or why not?

42a. How sexual and how sensual are you? If involved with someone, how sexual and how sensual is your partner? How sexual and how sensual do/did you feel around your partner?

42b. How does this chemistry (or lack thereof) affect other areas of your life?

43a. Do you worry about money? What does your rational mind tell you about money? What does your intuition whisper to you? If your rational mind is right, what do you need to do? If your intuition is right, what do you need to do?

43b. Brainstorm ways of reconciling your intuition and rational mind if they are, in fact, both right about money. In a "both/and" universe, how can you balance both sides?

44a. Who do you envy and why?

44b. What does your envy tell you about your own longings and abilities? How could you rephrase your envy into a powerful intention for your own success and happiness?

45. Which fairy tale character, myth, or archetype do you most resonate with and why? What does your answer tell you about themes, challenges and choices in your life?

46a. What recurring dreams, daydreams or fantasies have you had recently and/or over the course of your life?

46b. What themes, challenges and choices do these dreams, daydreams or fantasies highlight?

47a. In which ways is your journey a spiral journey? Which people, themes or situations have recurred periodically at different levels throughout your life?

47b. From your current perspective, which level are you at now? How would the next level look and feel to you?

48. Do you love to dance? Why or why not? What does dancing represent for you? How is your attitude towards dance a metaphor for your life?

49a. What kind of relationships do you have with chocolate, wine, spirits (hard alcohol and/or ephemeral beings), and sex? What do these relationships represent for you?

49b. Of these relationships with chocolate, wine, spirits and sex, which brings you the greatest challenges? Which offers the greatest rewards? Which do you need to leave behind or process in a different way?

50. If you knew you had all the money you need to thrive, what would you do? How would you be?

51. Describe any love/hate dynamics between you and money.

52. If you had a magic wand, how would you use it? What does your answer tell you about your attitude towards wishes, hopes and dreams?

53. If you had a magic wand, how often would you use it? Would you really use it that seldom or often, or does this just seem like the obvious or expected answer? What rules or restrictions would govern your use of a magic wand?

54. Do you believe in miracles? Why or why not?

55. Do you believe in God, Goddess, The Force, The Universe, Something or Nothing else? Why or why not? How intimately do you feel connected to the Mystery of Life?

56a. How comfortable are you with giving or receiving pleasure during sexual encounters? Does it depend on the person, or does this level of comfort or discomfort remain constant in you regardless of partner?

56b. What might your answers reveal about your inner guidelines for giving or receiving in life?

57. What's your favorite fabric or material? Which qualities do you love about it? In which ways are you like or unlike these qualities?

58. How do you feel about the Goddess? What does your answer suggest about your relationship to the Divine Feminine in yourself or others?

59. How do you feel about witches, hags and crones? What does your answer suggest about your relationship to the Dark Feminine or the Wild Feminine?

60. How do you feel about the Divine Masculine? Where does this show up in your life and relationships? Where do you feel a sense of lack or oppression?

61a. How do you feel about children - your own and in general?

61b. In which ways does your relationship with your children and/or the idea of children play out in other areas of life? (At work? In your creative process? In your intimate relationships?)

61c. In which areas do you need to cultivate more balance related to this theme of children?

62. In which ways does your inner child feel neglected or unloved? How could you establish a stronger connection with this young, playful, wounded part of you?

63a. How do you feel about abandonment? When have you felt abandoned? When have you abandoned someone else?

63b. In which ways do your feelings about abandonment affect your ability to live with "wild abandon"? What lines do you draw between what you consider appropriate or inappropriate desires?

64. At what age do you consider "desire" to be appropriate or inappropriate? How did you determine this age?

65. When have you felt betrayed by someone else? What did you learn (or continue learning) from this experience and dynamic?

66. When have you betrayed someone else? In which ways was this betrayal of someone else also a betrayal or honoring of your truest self?

67. Considering abandonment and betrayal as themes in your life, how have these experiences related to you being "pushed out of the nest" or you pushing someone else out of the nest, in order to fly?

68a. What "if only" statements do you find yourself making? (i.e. "If only I had more money, I would ___." "If only I were healed, I'd ____.") What larger themes and longings do these "if only" statements suggest?

69b. How could you bring more of your "if only" statements into your lived reality? (i.e. What small shifts or habits remind you of having more money, better health, etc.?)

70. In what ways do you require someone else to change in order for you to be happy? What does happiness require of you?

71. When you feel an unexpected spark of attraction with someone, male or female, where does your mind tend to go? What might this tell you about your approach to life and love?

72. What, if any, intimacy issues do you have? How do your and/or what you perceive as other people's intimacy issues affect your relationships?

73. What would make you more comfortable with intimacy? What do you need in order to feel safe in a relationship?

74. Which relationships in your life feel safe to you? Which relationships in your life feel unsafe? What do you make of these lists? What, if any, patterns do your answers reveal?

75. What do you consider sacred? What feels like a desecration? What insights do your answers provide into life patterns, expectation, and choices?

76. How do you feel about monogamy? How have issues related to monogamy supported or undermined your life?

77. Are you better at beginning or finishing creative projects? How does this pattern play out in other areas of life?

78. In which ways do you fulfill the role of mother or father? In which ways do you need more mothering and fathering? What small steps can you take to create more balance in this area?

79a. What do you associate with the terms "womb," "gestation" and "birth"? List all the ideas each term brings to mind.

79b. What insights do your answers offer?

80a. With names, photos, or family tree, ponder and describe how your lineage runs through your life. How do your life challenges represent larger patterns in need of healing?

80b. How does this awareness of generational patterns shift your attitude and healing strategy?

81. What's your relationship with caffeine? Do you feel comfortable with this relationship? How does it restrict, benefit, shame, enhance, or sabotage you?

82. When you get a creative idea, do you run with it? Tuck it away for a rainy day? Talk yourself out of it or try to suppress it? How do you feel about your responses? What do they suggest about your creative process?

83. What do you wish you could do? What support would you need in order to feel confident in your ability to do this? Which small steps might open possibilities for you?

84. How do you begin your day? Do your first actions make you feel honored and supported? How might your first actions set a more positive course for your day?

85. How do you end your day? Do your last actions make you feel honored and supported? How might your last actions set a more positive course for your sleep and dreams?

86. Do you speak your truth? Why or why not? If you can't speak your truth out loud to someone, what other ways can you express these thoughts and energies?

87. How do you move excess energy through your mind and body? Are you satisfied with these methods? If not, what are you willing to experiment with to see if it works better?

88. How do you feel after an orgasm? Besides sex, what other things feel "orgasmic" to you? What hangups or potential openings do your answers suggest for you?

89. What does "sovereignty" mean to you? Do you consider this a political, spiritual, or personal concept? Do you feel sovereign? Why or why not?

90. How does desire relate to creativity?

91a. What do you most desire to create? Why?

91b. What do you most desire to receive? Why?

92. What does your primal inner knowing tell you that you need in life? How can you address these needs? What small step(s) can you take towards listening to and honoring your primal inner knowing?

93. Open your favorite book to a "random" page and see where your eyes fall on that page. Alternatively, pull an oracle card, Rune, tarot card, or throw coins for the I Ching. Feel first, before looking up "official" meanings. What message(s) are you receiving? You can make this a daily practice to align with the Creative Energy flowing in and through your Second Chakra.

94. What signs, song lyrics, or synchronicities have you noticed lately? Have you had any recurring "random" thoughts, conversations or dreams? What do you hope these mean?

95. Use this page to write an introduction or poem, to paint a picture or make a collage that represents your most creative, joyful inner being. Love, honor and cherish this part of you. Live on intimate terms with your sacred self. Thou art that.

This journal ends here, but beyond the journal, beyond your symptoms, your journey continues. I invite you to glance through your questions and answers. How have you changed? What core truths did you discover about yourself? If you feel so led, you can find more information and intuitive coaching support from me at asklaurabruno.com. Whatever your path, I wish you peace, joy and wisdom.

Blessings and healing,

Laura Bruno

Made in the USA
Monee, IL
08 November 2020